Dichos de mi Padre

Sayings of my Father

Geneva Maria Escobedo

Dichos de mi Padre

SAYINGS OF MY FATHER

Latino Book Publisher
Mesa, Arizona 2017

FIRST EDITION | 2017
Book design: Yolie Hernandez (azbookdesigner@icloud.com)
Text copyright © 2017 by Geneva Maria Escobedo

Latino Book Publisher
An imprint of the Hispanic Institute of Social Issues
PO Box 50553
Mesa, Arizona 85208-0028
(480) 646-9401 | hisi.org | info@hisi.org

Escobedo, Geneva Maria
Dichos de mi Padre- Sayings of my Father / Geneva Maria Escobedo

ISBN-13: 978-1-936885-23-7

Manufactured in the United States of America.
1 2 3 4 5 6 7 8 9 10

Dedication

To my parents and grandparents:

My father, Pedro Luna Escobedo, Jr., who passed on June 10, 2001 at age 76.

My mother, Brijida Barela Escobedo, who remains a source of strength for me.

My paternal grandfather, Pedro Escobedo, Sr., who taught me the value of hard work.

My paternal grandmother, Maria Luna Escobedo, the true source of the *dichos* contained in this book. She instilled in me the importance of honoring my Mexican heritage and maintaining my Spanish language.

Special Thanks

To my cousins, Romana Escobedo Forsythe (eldest daughter of my Tío Julio Escobedo). She entered into rest on October 25, 2011; Federico "Lico" Escobedo (son of Tío Tomás), and Jessie Escobedo Formica (daughter of Tío Tomás). I thank them for the stories they shared about our family history.

Contents

Photo with Dad—age 24 when I started collecting the dichos, 1973.

Introduction

Over the course of 20 years, when I visited my parents on weekends and holidays and up until my father's death, I would take my little journal and jot down a *dicho* that my father shared during our many conversations.

Since my father passed in 2001, I made several attempts to write this book. It has been an intriguing journey as a novice writer. There were times that the stories blossomed effortlessly, and other times when I could not maintain my focus. I received input from family members, writing partners and friends. I started writing this book in 2006. I have been through numerous edits and all the while, my intentions to complete it remained strong.

It was during a writing exercise at a monthly meeting of my women's writing group, "Sowing the Seeds," in 2006, that I received the "kick" I needed to develop the structure of my manuscript and begin to shape the stories. During a meditative session, the following vision appeared:

There is a cool afternoon breeze flowing through the ramada of my Grandma Maria's casita. Abuelita and Papá sit next to each other, chatting away while eating the sweet purple grapes hanging from the vines that surround the ramada Grandpa Pedro built.

"I don't know what's holding mijita up from writing that book she's talked about for years," Papá says.

"Don't worry mijo. She needs to feel the moment. It's in her heart to get it written and she'll do it," abuelita says without concern.

Papá believes that the stories and values his mamá passed on to him need to be shared with younger generations. Papá is contemplating how he might be of help.

"Shall I enter her dreams? Perhaps if she has me on her mind she'll quit procrastinating. I remember her many visits when I was alive. She was so enthusiastic about writing all my *dichos* down. She said she'd pull them all together in a book."

Abuelita interrupts my dad's thoughts. She explains that their spirits will surround me, and that she's sure the book will be completed. She knows it will bring the family together. The *dichos* she passed on to her son will not go unnoticed. She relaxes. The sun has set. As darkness comes, she sees her loved ones preparing for sleep. She decides she'll enter my dreams to give me that little push.

What is a dicho?

A *dicho* is a philosophical saying handed down from one generation to another that gives meaning to life and reinforces family values. *Dichos* are proverbs or Latino/Mexican folk wisdom. *Dichos* are quite common in Spanish-speaking cultures. Mom and dad spoke about *dichos* while I was growing up. I began to pay attention to their cultural value while I was in college. I appreciate them more now that my father is gone.

Each chapter in this book begins with a *dicho* in Spanish, its translation in English, and a story to relay its meaning or lesson. Some are humorous, others are sad. Interpret them any way you wish. Hand them down to your children; discuss them with your grandchildren. Create your own special *dichos*. So, I begin with 20 of my favorite *dichos* and related stories...

Cada chango en su columpio

(Every monkey chooses his own swing)

Throughout our lives, we make many choices—some good, some bad. Dad always preached to us about making smart choices—do well in school, mind your mother, choose good friends, and when and if you decide to marry, choose a good partner.

I recall him giving me advice not to get married. He would say, *"No te cases mijita. ¿Para qué quieres problemas?"* (Don't get married, my daughter. Why do you want problems?) Being the only girl in the family and raised Catholic in a traditional Mexican home, this message was unusual. Most girls from my small town of Safford, Arizona not only thought about getting married and having children, but were encouraged to do so at a young age. The fact that my father didn't buy into that norm and didn't encourage it, gave me the freedom to think about the swings I wanted to experience.

The swing I chose was to pursue a college degree. I am the only member of my immediate family to achieve this. I have also made it my life's mission to encourage and help others succeed in college.

I eventually got married at the ripe age of 31. I thought I chose a good partner and although we shared many happy years together, our lives grew apart. After 18 years together, we eventually chose to climb a different swing.

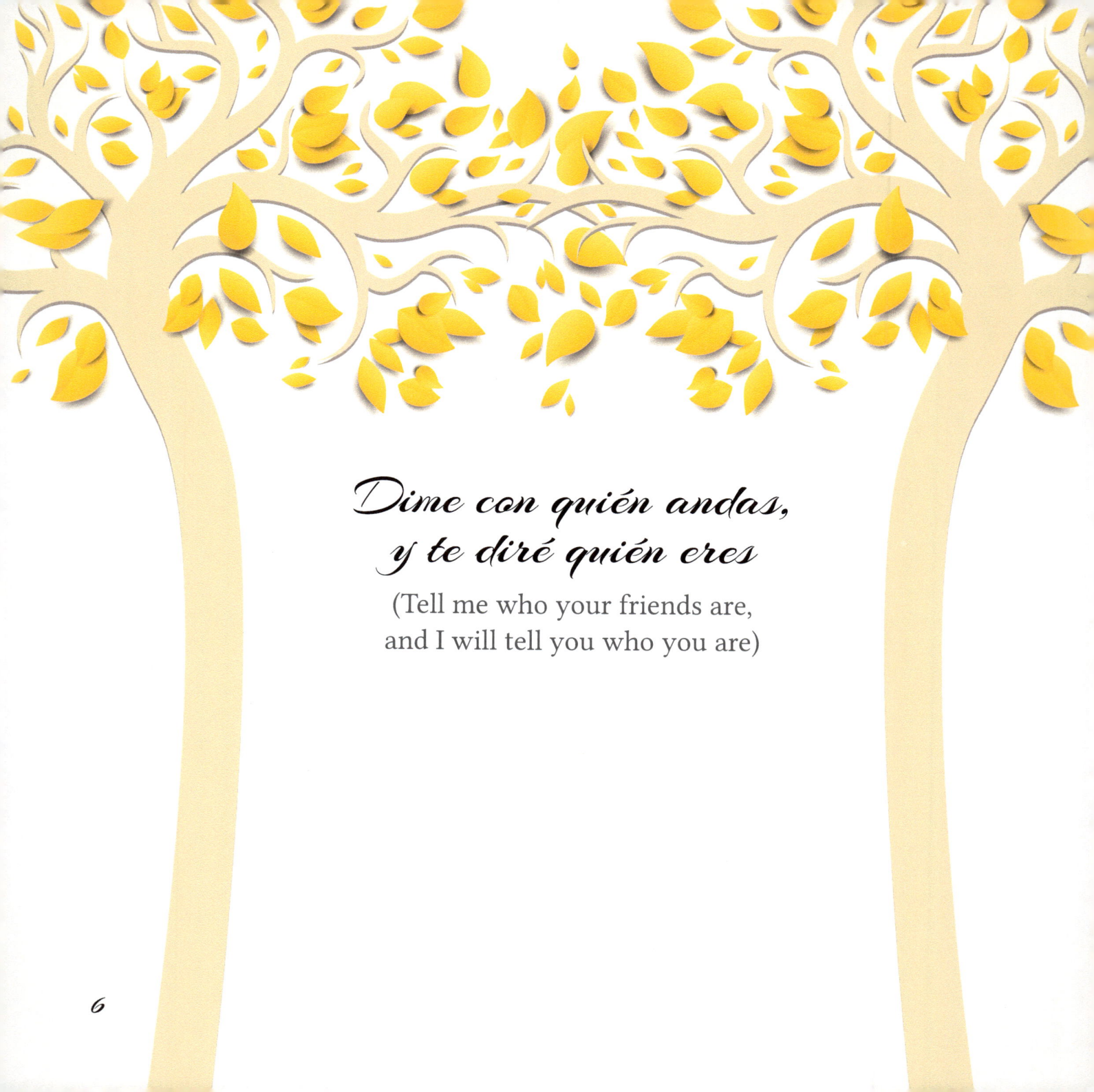

Dime con quién andas,
y te diré quién eres

(Tell me who your friends are,
and I will tell you who you are)

At times, we are judged by the type of people we surround ourselves with. My parents wanted our friends to come from well-respected, families. When my brothers hung out with troublemakers, dad would have a fit. He wanted them to be honest, not steal and to demonstrate good manners at all times. He said, "If you spend your time with hoodlums, then people will think you are one of them."

The conversations between my dad and brothers about their selection of friends greatly influenced how I saw myself. They helped shape my thinking about the type of woman I wanted to become. I was quite sheltered and wanted to please my parents. I became very goal-oriented, studious, and chose to befriend a Chinese classmate, Donna Hom, who was quiet like me. She helped me achieve academically, and when we graduated from high school with scholarships, we were more than ready to attend college.

This particular *dicho* still resonates with me. I make a conscious choice to surround myself with positive, lifelong learners who support me and challenge me to grow in numerous ways.

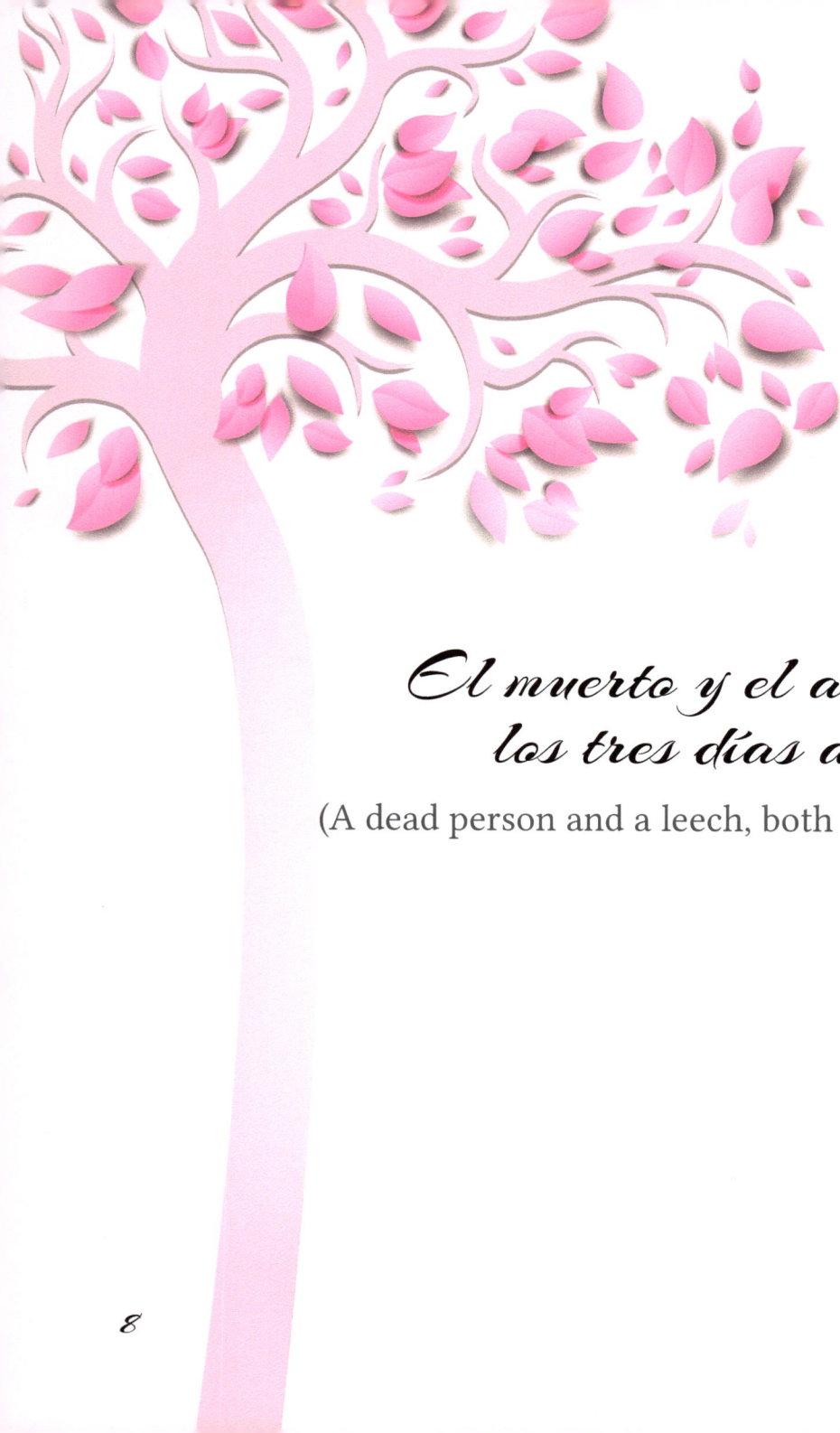

El muerto y el arrimado a los tres días apestan

(A dead person and a leech, both stink after three days)

Dicho 3

In large Mexican families there are often family members who ask for a helping hand. It can be a cousin, a brother-in-law or a friend of the family. My parents lived a Christian life and did not turn away family members who needed help. When my Aunt Nellie was very ill, my mother and her siblings each took one of her children until my aunt recovered. We were fortunate to have Richard stay with us six months, and to this day I consider him a brother.

My parents also took in Richard's older sister, Julie, when she was in high school. My grandmother raised her and when her widowed son decided to move to California for a new job, Grandmother went with him to help raise his three children. Julie did not want to move and it was important for her to graduate from Safford High School. I was elated that I would finally have a sister. She lived with us for four years until she married. She is my sister-cousin and a source of strength for me. She was someone I could share my dreams with, vent with when my brothers drove me nuts, and helped me with the cooking and cleaning.

I am proud that my parents were such giving people and helped others in need. But there was a time when giving a helping hand became cumbersome. It happened when my brother Eddie was discharged from the Army. He brought home a blonde, blue-eyed Army buddy named Don. What started out as a short visit turned into a one-year stay. Don didn't have a family and he had no idea where to go or what to do with his life. Dad encouraged him to get a job and mom made sure he ate well.

He was a very quiet individual but did not maintain good hygiene. This bothered Mom quite a bit because she raised us to keep ourselves clean, and to keep our home clean and clutter free. She was torn between helping this sad orphan and giving him the boot.

He finally left on his own and we did not hear from him for quite some time. A few years after he left and while I was in college, I learned that my mother was hospitalized because of an allergic reaction to sulfa. I rushed to the hospital and to my surprise, Don came to check in on mom. He told her how much he appreciated her help during his time of need and that he was doing fine.

Tiene las pulgas muy cerca

(The fleas are too close to the skin; he/she has a short fuse)

In our extended family, we have a wide array of personalities. Some of us get along swimmingly, and others clash and can create drama.

My dad would share stories about his sisters. Two of his elder sisters were close in age and had a lot in common. His youngest sister, Beatrice, also called *"Tichi,"* was an independent spirit. She had a strong personality and at times would get upset if things did not go her way.

What grandma meant when she said, *"tiene las pulgas muy cerca,"* was that Aunt Beatrice could easily lose her temper. Abuelita told my dad, *"tienes que tocarla con un palito"* (you have to touch her softly with a little stick).

This *dicho* spoke to how grandma dealt with family members or friends who were a little more sensitive than others. Her lesson is one of tolerance, respect and understanding.

How many people in your life can you relate to with this *dicho*? A spouse? A friend? A co-worker? Your boss? Think about it!

Hasta a la profesora se le queman los libros

(No matter how many books you have read or how educated you are, there are times when your common sense can go out the window)

My parents stressed the value of education. As the eldest and only daughter in the family, I knew I had to set an example for my younger brothers. I loved to read, attend school and strived to attain good grades.

After high school, I attended the local community college and earned my associate's degree in business. It paved the way to greater achievements, and prepared me to leave my small hometown to spread my wings in the big city of Phoenix.

I worked for six years in Phoenix and then decided to return to college for my bachelor's degree. The three years prior to applying for admission to Arizona State University, I worked for Chicanos Por La Causa, a community development corporation dedicated to empowering the Hispanic community in the areas of health, education, housing and economic development. Chicanos Por La Causa has become one of the most prominent community development corporations in the United States, and has served as a model for other communities. The three years I worked there proved to be eye-opening in terms of community politics, social services and diversity issues.

My career since earning my undergraduate degree in Business Administration has taken me on many journeys, all of which have been fulfilling—from working as a human resources professional for a large telecommunications company, to fundraising, to a 29-year career in higher education.

Despite my educational and professional accomplishments, my family never hesitates to keep me grounded. They remind me that no matter how many books I read and how much education I have, I can still "mess up" when it comes to everyday tasks. For example, I struggle with connecting electronic devices (even though I can read directions). I occasionally turn on the coffee pot without adding the ground coffee beans, and forget where I left my keys.

My brother Ben was painting my bedroom a few years ago and I offered to help paint the door. He later told me, "Sis, you are smart in many ways, but you don't know how to paint!"

La mentira luce mientras
que la verdad llega

(Beware of your lies because the truth will be revealed)

Have you ever told a lie? Sure you have. We all do at one time or another. Sometimes we justify "little white lies" so we won't hurt someone's feelings. For example, telling someone they look great in their new pair of jeans, when they really don't.

Growing up with four brothers, any one of us was caught in a lie at one point or another. The truth came out eventually. Mom and Dad could tell just by looking into our eyes. My brother Eddie was the defiant one; he was quite stubborn and challenged our parents on all fronts. From wearing sloppy clothes, not brushing his teeth, to cutting classes and not doing his homework. My baby brother, "Petie" (Pedro Escobedo III), was quiet and sneaky. He lied about throwing rocks at the neighbor's cat. Mom found out later after a brief visit with Frances, the next door neighbor.

Our parents taught us that when you lie, you hurt yourself more than the person you lied to. They relayed to us that we must be honorable and trustworthy, and that when you lie, trust is lost. To regain that trust takes a great deal of effort, and if your lie is a big one, you may lose a friend forever. Not everyone forgives easily.

Mom told me about a lie she caught my dad in. One time he went to the local western store and a 5X Beaver hat caught his eye, however, the price was $550. The sales lady offered a 50% discount and he decided to purchase it, but without my mother's knowledge. He hid the hat in the closet for a few months. Mother eventually found it and confronted him. They argued for a while, but the bottom line was that he wanted it, he worked for it, and he was going to keep it!

Now that my brothers and I are parents and grandparents, we have passed on the importance of refraining from lying. And the cycle continues...

El que no conoce a Dios, a
cualquier santo adora

(He who does not believe in God adores any idol)

Dicho 7

Grandma Maria was a woman of faith. She believed in the Lord, prayed to the saints and was a devout Catholic. She passed her faith on to my father. She felt strongly about living a Christian life and not believing in false prophets who could lead you down the wrong path.

Up until I was six years old, I lived in a small Mexican-American community called Solomonville, Arizona where my dad was raised. I loved going to the little "Virgen de Guadalupe" church for Sunday mass with my grandma and my aunt/godmother, Isabel (my dad's older sister). It is a quaint, spiritual place with a strong faith community. Mom and Dad were married in this little church. My brothers Tony, Eddie, Ben and I were baptized there. To this day, this church remains a special place.

I have lived a Catholic life but did stray during my 20's, however, never to the point where I adored a false idol. I pray the rosary and speak to the Virgen de Guadalupe, who is a source of empowerment for me. I also pray to Saint Anne, Saint Francis of Assisi and the Holy Spirit. I ask them to protect my loved ones from harm and help those in need of healing. Prayer is powerful!

Del dicho al hecho, hay un gran trecho

(What you say you will do and what you actually
do requires work and commitment)

Keeping your word and being your word is a virtue I have aspired to all my life. The many lessons my parents taught me are reflected in the following statements that were shared while I was growing up:

"When you say you will do something, stick to it no matter what."

"Keeping your word is important to others—keep it so you don't lose their trust."

"There will be times when it may seem that you can't complete what you set out to do— just take it in small steps and stay on track."

My goal after graduating from high school was to attend college. I went to our local community college because it was close to home and affordable. I earned my associate's degree with honors.

My second goal was to leave the small town I grew up in and make my mark in the big city. I shared my dream of being a professional woman at a large company with my classmates, family and friends. After graduating from Eastern Arizona College I was recruited by The Arizona Bank, in Phoenix, and was offered my first professional position as Executive Secretary to the Vice President of the International Department. It was traditional work for a young woman at the time (1969), but it was a path to greater things.

Thanks to my parents and grandparents, I spoke Spanish at home. Knowing this language helped me land the job, and I enjoyed communicating in Spanish with staff at various Mexican banks. I improved my Spanish speaking and writing skills by taking classes offered by bank professionals who grew up in Mexico.

However, an associate's degree in Business was not enough. I knew I had to obtain my bachelor's degree to achieve higher level positions. I told my family that I would go to Arizona State University and complete my degree, no matter how long it took. After six years of working for two corporations and a non-profit organization, I sold my car, got financial aid, bought a bike and moved to an inexpensive apartment near the main campus of Arizona State University, in Tempe.

It took me three years to complete my bachelor's degree, and I later completed a Master's in Business Administration. Through working in various positions, I began to make my mark. As Director of Arizona State University's Downtown Center (during the 1990's), I created the Non-Profit Management Institute. This collaborative project continues operating to this day. I was the founding president of Arizona State University's Hispanic Business Alumni, and helped raise funds to develop a scholarship program. In my role as the Title V Grant Program Director at Pima Community College, I organized a state-wide conference on developmental education, where issues regarding underprepared college students were addressed.

I relay these humble accomplishments to emphasize that when you state you will do something, commit to it and see it through to the end. You will never know how much impact you will have on others.

Dichos populares
Popular sayings

Amores de lejos son amores de pendejos

(Long-distance love relationships are for idiots)

Después de un buen servicio, un mal pago

(After giving good service, you get poor payment)

Debo no niego, pago no tengo

(I don't deny I owe, but I can't pay)

Ojos que no ven, corazón que no siente

(What your eyes cannot see, your heart cannot feel)

Cada quien tiene sus costumbres. Y el que será así, desde la cuna comienza.

(Everyone has their habits and are formed since birth)

*De grano en grano se llena
la gallina el buche*

(Little by little you accomplish your goal)

Among Dad's many lessons, his example of working hard and giving maximum effort is the lesson I saw him model every day. Laziness was not an option in our home. He directed my brothers and I to scrub walls, mop floors, clean windows and do dishes as a regular part of our routine.

His was a family of cotton farmers. Up until I was about eight years old, Dad worked at the Larsen Farms in Safford, Arizona. He took the opportunity to earn more money and accepted a job with the Phelps Dodge Morenci Copper Company.

I'll never forget the Saturday Dad took me, brother Tony and brother Eddie to pick cotton. We were eight, seven and six years old, respectively. "I'm going to teach you how to work and earn money," he said. He took us to the Larsen Farms and gave us each a burlap sack. He told us to go down a row, pick the cotton off the bushes and place it in the sack. When you are done, he added, the boss will weigh your sack and pay you accordingly. In my mind I thought I'd earn quite a bit—at least $10.

My two brothers immediately made it a competition. "I bet I'll fill up my sack first," yelled Tony. Eddie, not to be undone, proclaimed, "We'll see about that. I'm faster!" I, on the other hand, took my time filling the burlap sack one cotton ball at a time. I started a rhythm for picking, moving down one row and then to the next, trying not to leave any cotton pods on the bush. I ignored my brothers and moved diligently and methodically.

What seemed like a full day of hard work turned out to less than an hour or so. Dad called us to bring in our sacks and get them weighed. The three of us were excited. We each earned about fifty cents, but our sacks were not full. Although we were disappointed that we didn't earn what we expected, Dad helped us realize that no matter what kind of work you do, you need to take your time and do it well. "Apply yourself and take pride in what you do," he stated.

*Vale más un pájaro en la
mano que dos volando.*

(One bird in your hand is worth more than two birds flying)

*T*his *dicho* speaks to being content with what you have and not to get too greedy. In our fast-paced world, we get wrapped up in climbing up the promotional ladder for more money, more prestige and to make greater contributions through these highly responsible roles.

Does it really matter that we have an enormous home, the latest automobile model, or the finest clothes?

My parents were raised with little financial means. They lived simply and worked hard all their lives. Mom's family of 12, with my widowed grandmother the head of household, required everyone to pitch in so they could eat and take care of the home. Dad's family of eight lived in a tiny two-bedroom house. They raised an extensive garden that helped feed everyone. The way they lived their lives impacted my thinking about the importance of supporting family, and that material possessions are not a substitute for happiness.

Coming from a low-income family, I appreciate my middle class life. I have enough money to not only meet my daily living expenses, but to take memorable vacations from time to time.

I have no desire to be rich. What I have in my hands now creates contentment and peace. One bird is enough.

Lágrimas de borracho son como lágrimas de perro, se salen sin sentir

(A drunkard's tears are like a dog's tears; they appear without sincerity)

I suspect that Grandma Maria witnessed the tears of a drunkard many times. She said they were not tears of remorse. She often thought that a drunkard's tears were meaningless and not genuine. "They cry because they feel sorry for themselves or regret hurting their loved ones," she said.

I am not sure if this is entirely true. The men in my Mexican-American family were taught not to cry. It could be that when they got inebriated, all the pent-up emotions (sadness, regret, anger, disappointment) tumbled down in the form of sobs. Not a pretty picture from a sober woman's perspective. I find it intolerable to be around drunks. and I don't want to be a witness to these types of *"lágrimas."*

Rodando se encuentran las piedras

(Literal: The rolling stones find each other and connect
Translation: As we move along through life we connect with others)

Dicho 12

This *dicho* speaks to how individuals find each other during life's journeys. Who we meet as we progress through life can become our future spouse, a life-long friend, a mentor or a child who makes a difference in our life.

I believe we meet individuals who are meant to give us a life lesson or who inspire us with a message we desperately need to hear. Sometimes we meet someone who is not a positive influence but teaches us what we must avoid in the future.

In my journey as a writer, I have met men and women who inspire me, share writing techniques or resources and who spend valuable time critiquing my work. A friend of mine states, "There are no accidents." I take this to mean that we are supposed to run into certain people or be part of particular events for a reason.

Rodando means wondering or moving right along. The *piedras* we encounter along the way can be people, events, animals or places. One of my most profound events was joining my friend Ilynn Adler at a summer retreat in Abiquiu, New Mexico. We searched for a place where we could heal and further explore our spirituality. We found the perfect workshop called "The Spirituality of Brokenness." The timing could not have been better.

I hiked, wrote, read, prayed, practiced yoga, and reflected and conversed with an amazing mix of people. By getting away from my troubles and anxiety, I found peace and inner healing. The poem below describes my experience.

The Healing Place
Blue mountain vistas stand out against the sky.
Clouds overhead slowly release the gift of
welcomed moisture to this dry land

Generous breezes flow upon my face,
opening the wounds I must see.
I've come to the perfect healing place.

Red and amber mesas stand firm despite the years
of lines and wrinkles created by Mother Nature.
I see parts of me in them. Their strength helps me move on.

Two golden birds romp among the branches of
a pine tree. They bring hope that I will one day
unite with my soul mate.

The leaves of many cottonwoods glisten and
flutter like the wings of a butterfly.
They bend to the arroyo below as if saying,
We honor you. Your stream of water sustains us.
Thank you for this blessing.

The healing place brings me respite and peace.
Opens my mind, heart and soul. Allows it's
energy to engulf me.

I set aside my fears, anxiety, and pain. I am one
with the healing place.

I look forward to continuing my *rodando* and encountering people who I am meant to meet and with whom I can gain new perspectives and lessons.

Más dichos populares
More popular sayings

No hay loco que coma lumbre

(There is not a crazy person who would eat fire)

Con hilo y un palito, todo se compone

(With a piece of thread and a little stick, you can fix anything)

Anda como burro sin mecate. No tiene rienda.

(He runs around like a donkey without a rope. He has no restraint.)

Está más pobre que un chaleco sin botones

(He is as poor as a vest without buttons)

Si no hubiera gusto, pobre de nosotros
los feos que nos tiraban a un lado.

(If there were no desires, pity the ugly ones who would be thrown aside.)

Dios castiga sin palo y sin cuarta

(God punishes without using a stick or a whip)

Dicho 13

Growing up Catholic, I learned about mortal sins and venial sins. Mortal sins are grave offenses like killing and stealing. Venial sins are telling little white lies and having bad thoughts.

I would go to confession regularly, and my usual punishment for disobeying my parents or fighting with my brothers was an "Our Father" and ten "Hail Mary's." As I matured, I learned that punishment can come in many forms. You can lose a friend if you don't treat them well. This can hurt more than if someone slapped you in the face.

Grandma would say, *"Te va a castigar Dios si no te portas bien"* (God will punish you if you don't behave well). I didn't understand that the worst punishment for doing something wrong was not getting a paddling; it was how horrible one can feel when we hurt someone else. Those moments of agony, feeling guilty and not feeling great about yourself are a far tougher punishment than getting an old-fashioned whipping.

Hablando se entienden las cosas

(By communicating, one understands)

Dicho 14

*H*ealthy relationships require effective and open communication. My parents' secret to a 52-year marriage was to never go to bed angry with each other. They got whatever they needed to "off their chest," and gave each other a hug or a soft touch before they went to sleep. When they argued in the presence of my brothers, it was done respectfully, and when they each had their say (even though there was a difference of opinion), it often ended in laughter.

Dad expressed that if we don't share our feelings or listen to what others have to say, we won't fully understand what is going on. He said, "Don't be afraid to say what's on your mind. Let people know why you are sad, angry or disappointed." This opens the door to greater understanding, compromise if necessary, or clarification.

Dad lived these words at home and at work. His employees respected him and enjoyed working for him.

No metas pobres en trabajos

(Don't involve others in your troubles)

Dicho 15

My *padrecito* was a man who took care of his family and helped relatives in need. He believed that you should take care of your own business and not get involved in other people's problems.

He and mom communicated well, and although they would disagree on how to resolve a situation, they talked it out until they reached a satisfactory conclusion. On one occasion, they were at their wits end on how to pay all the bills. With five children to feed and clothe, plus a house payment, Dad's salary at the copper mine and Mom's part-time job, were barely enough to make ends meet.

This was sometimes hard for Dad. He was proud and he was committed to being a good provider. I recall one bothersome argument when I was about 15 years old. I had a small savings account from the house cleaning and babysitting I did for the neighbor across the street. I had a balance of $90.

While Mom and Dad were arguing in the kitchen about their financial woes, I wrote a note to Dad and left it on his dresser. It said: "Please don't fight. I will give you my $90 to help pay the bills."

When Dad saw the note he called me over. He said, "*Mijita*, you've worked hard for your money. I won't take it. Your mom and I will work this out. It will be okay."

I sensed that he was embarrassed for airing out his frustrations and causing me to worry about family finances. I'll never forget that moment, and do my best not to involve others in my troubles.

No hay mal que por bien no venga

(Bad luck is always followed by goodness)

Dicho 16

When Dad was quite ill with Parkinson's and congenital heart disease the last three years of his life, Mom was working part-time and raising her grandson. Little Benji is my third brother's son. His mom abandoned him at six months and Mom and Dad raised him. He was the cutest bundle of joy. You just wanted to wrap your arms around him and keep him safe.

Little Benji was a blessing for Dad because he brought him laughter, and gave him a reason to get up each morning no matter how ill he felt. Benji would tease Dad, play games with him and give him lots of hugs. Benji was a year-old when Dad passed.

After his passing, Benji helped Mom through her grief and gave her purpose. "I didn't have time to feel sorry for myself," she stated. "I had this little boy to raise. He made it easier for me to handle the loss," she added.

There are times in life when the unexpected happens—when you are faced with adversity. Mom taught us to pray daily, not only to thank the Lord for our blessings, but to ask for the strength to conquer our fears and overcome barriers. She and dad believed that when tragedy or disappointment occurs it would always be followed by something good. There are lessons to be learned from the tough times, and you can count on life balancing itself out.

Hace las cosas al grito y al panzaso

(Literal translation: He accomplishes things by screaming and banging his tummy against things. He accomplishes things any which way)

D ad was somewhat obsessive about neatness and cleanliness. He taught us to scrub floors on our knees, wash windows, clean walls and toilets, wash dishes and pull weeds. He expected us to do a quality job on all our tasks, and inspected our work after we finished. If it wasn't up to his standards, we had to start over again. Streaky windows were his pet peeve!

My middle brother, Eddie, had a rough time adhering to Dad's standards. His sloppy work caused numerous lectures. Eddie was in a world of his own. He was smart, funny and it didn't matter what he wore or what he looked like. He usually dressed in faded jeans, stained t-shirts, and his famous "biker" boots. They had black thick soles and left scuff marks on the floors.

The furthest thing from his mind was quality work or handing in exceptional school work. He completed his work, but it wasn't with intensity or with an interest in doing his absolute best. He didn't think too much about excelling in high school although we all knew he could get A's. His way of being was, "I'll finish it and get it over with so I can go on to the next thing."

Brother Eddie grew up to become a hard worker at the copper mines in Morenci. He retired after 30 years. He has a gentle giving heart and is a joy to be with. I can always count on laughing my head off with him when we get together. He raised three children and has 13 grandchildren. He is the only one of our immediate family whose marriage remains intact. I am so proud of him and his wife for overcoming challenges and remaining committed to their marriage.

As I reflect on this *dicho*, I recall how much the lesson of doing your best is ingrained in me. I apply it to my writing—reviewing, revising, editing, and re-visioning until my stories and poems are almost perfect.

Dos agujas no se pican

(Two individuals with the same personality
often don't experience conflict)

Individuals with similar personalities usually get along swimmingly. Two people who are opposites can at times experience conflict. Siblings who are as different as night and day can prick each other if their views on a controversial topic are miles apart from each other's or if they don't see a situation in the same way.

Two members of my family are very negative—they have similar personalities. When they get together they feed each other's negativity. They can talk for hours about the unrest in the world, murders and mayhem that they saw in the news, who just got divorced, or who's children are in trouble and why. They enjoy each other's company because they are on the same wave length.

On the other hand, two other family members have a positive view on life. They have lively conversations and discuss their vision for the future, their recent successes and who they have encountered or read about that has influenced them.

Who in your life speaks to this *dicho*?

Es un parche mal pegado

(He/she is not a match for you)

Dicho 19

You learn a lot about male and female relationships from your parents, uncles, aunts, cousins and friends. I was fortunate to grow up with parents who were compatible and modeled commitment, love and dedication.

My parents celebrated their 50th wedding anniversary on March 20, 1999. It was a heartfelt ceremony to observe. At the time I was divorced as were three of my brothers. My brother Eddie and his wife have remained married and supportive of each other. It is a joy to see the love they have for each other and their commitment to their marriage. They are like "two peas in a pod."

When Dad talked about relationships that had ended, he would describe the couple as mismatched. For example, one of my brother's girlfriends caused a lot of drama. They didn't see things the same way nor did they have the same values. They argued way too much.

"El parche mal pegado" literally means a patch sewn on a garment that doesn't match or blend in. When thinking about people who don't seem to fit with each other, who comes to your mind? I must admit that most of the men I have dated over the years weren't a fit for me. It's been several years since my divorce, and I still have hope that there is a person out there who is a good match for me.

How many *"parches mal pegados"* have you come across in your life?

Qué bonito es hacer nada,
y luego descansar

(How beautiful it is to do nothing and after that, rest)

In our fast-paced, complex world it is often a challenge to find quiet time. Even when we are on vacation, we hop from place to place in an effort not to miss a thing. On a nine-day trip to Italy in 2009, we awoke by 6:00 a.m., toured four to six sites and had scheduled dinners at 7:00 p.m. I returned to the hotel room exhausted!

As I plan my next vacation, I envision myself on a beach sipping piña coladas and taking in the delicious breeze. After a power walk, I take a nap, then delve into the novel I selected.

We need to recharge at least once a year. What better way than to relax, take in nature, nap or just do nothing. No schedule... no phone... no email... just solitude and quiet. *¡Qué a gusto!*

Top: Escobedo family 1968. Standing L to R: Benjamin, Geneva, Anthony, Edward. Sitting L to R: Pedro Escobedo III, Brijida, and Pedro Escobedo, Jr.

Bottom left: Pedro Chavez and Maria Luna Escobedo Wedding Photo – April 23, 1916.

Bottom right: Pedro Escobedo, Jr. family photo circa 1925. Grandpa Pedro Escobedo, Grandma Maria Luna Escobedo. L to R: Isabel, Juanita, baby Carmen, and Cesario.

The Escobedo Family Branches

There are four branches of Escobedos and five generations of family. I have included four family trees at the end of this book. The first is the family tree of my great-grandparents, the second is of my grandparents, and the third is of my parents. The fourth family tree is that of Julio Escobedo, my great-uncle, and I included it because of the strong bonds between our families. Julio's third daughter, Nellie Escobedo Plasencio, was my Godmother. She was my mentor and supporter throughout my life. She passed away on All Saints Day, November 2, 2014.

My father greatly resembled Tío Julio in physical appearance and character. Tío Julio and dad were very close. After Tío Julio passed, my dad made sure Julio's wife, Tía Petra, was attended to. He would take her to the grocery store, run errands for her and at times, take her to church.

Grandpa Pedro and his brother Tomás worked together as farmers and businessmen. Tomás was quite successful and at times he and Grandpa did not see "eye to eye." Cousin Federico (Fred), the youngest son of Tomás and Maria Franco Escobedo shared the following story about great-uncle José and great-grandfather Cesario:

Grandpa Pedro and his brothers, Tomás and José, were returning home on a horse-driven wagon after a trip to Morenci, Arizona. They traveled from Safford to Morenci to sell the melons from their farm. As they were crossing a wash after arriving in San José (10 miles east of Safford), the horse was spooked. Suddenly, the wagon overturned and fell on top of Tío José. It was a fatal accident that killed Tío José on April 15, 1927. He left behind his wife, Maria Amado, and three children—Tony (killed in World War II in Iwo Jima), Carmen and Joe, Jr.

Cousin Fred recounted the story about my great-grandfather Cesario's funeral. The family contacted the priest at the Catholic Church in Solomonville, Arizona requesting to hold church services. The priest refused because my great-grandfather was not married to my great-grandmother. His sons and their friends marched to the church with rifles and demanded that the priest conduct a funeral mass. The priest did so with rifles pointed at him during the entire mass!

Tía Petra and Tío Julio Escobedo.

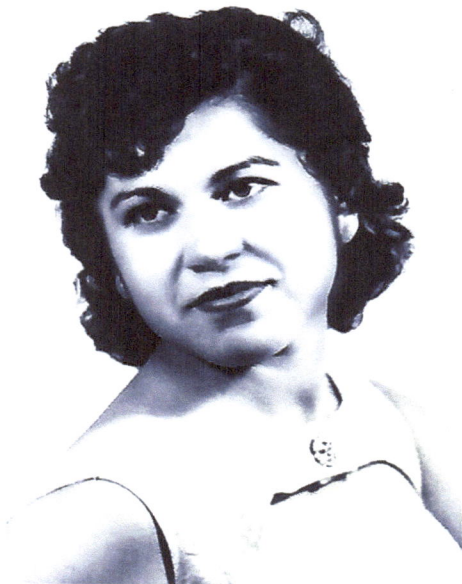
Juanita "Baby" Montoya Juarez.

Godmother Nellie Escobedo Plasencio.

Beatrice Escobedo Ruiz and
Isabel Escobedo Ornelas.

Mexican Immigrants

My grandmother, Maria Luna Escobedo, was born July 22, 1889 in a small pueblito in the state of Chihuahua, Mexico, not far from the city of Casas Grandes. She lived there during her formative years. My grandfather, Pedro Escobedo, was born on March 12, 1886 in a little town called El Carmen, set high in the mountains in Chihuahua. El Carmen was later renamed Ricardo Flores Magón. His siblings were Carmen, José, Tomás and Julio. They were a mix of indigenous Indian and Mexican as were their parents. My paternal great-grandfather, Cesario, was born in 1845 and sadly, lost his wife Romana Chavez Escobedo (born in Chile and immigrated to Mexico) at childbirth. He chose to journey from Mexico to the United States with his three sons, Pedro, José and Tomás, in search of a better life. It was a time when the borders were open and people crossed back and forth without concern. They left Carmen and Julio behind until they got settled. I was told the story of how my grandparents settled in Arizona countless times when I was a young girl.

During the time that my great-grandfather Cesario crossed the U.S.-Mexico border, five-year old Maria Luna (my paternal grandmother) and her mother, Tánislada (known as Doña Tánis), decided to travel to the United States through Ciudad Juarez (Chihuahua, Mexico), Texas and New Mexico in search of a new beginning. Great-grandmother, Doña Tánis, was a widow with two daughters. The eldest daughter, Rosalía, chose not to join them and remained in Mexico with her godmother. No one knows what happened to her.

These two brave women traveled on foot, with few belongings, but were armed with much more than material things. They had faith, hope and a strong will to survive. Along the way, they met Cesario and his sons. This unexpected meeting, which took place in Deming, New Mexico, marked the creation of a union that would last a lifetime. It signaled the blending of two families in search of a new start in the United States.

Tánislada and Cesario helped each other on their journey. Often, groups of immigrants traveled together for protection and to support one other along the way. My great-grandparents eventually settled in Solomonville, Arizona, a small rural farming community in southeastern Arizona. They merged their families without the formal bonds of marriage. Later, my great-uncle José returned to Mexico for Julio (age three) and great-aunt Carmen. With the families united, they continued their work on the farms growing watermelons, corn, chili and vegetables.

Tío Julio and my grandmother had a very close brother-sister relationship. They played for countless hours as small children and even wore each other's clothes. This family bond continues today through reunions of their children, grandchildren and great-grandchildren. My grandfather Pedro and grandmother Maria grew up as step-brother and step-sister.

The Escobedo's were expert farmers. They endured back-breaking work in the sweltering Arizona heat. When the work day ended, Cesario came home to a meal of freshly made flour tortillas and frijoles de la olla (freshly cooked whole beans). The evenings were spent telling stories of loved ones, tragedies, weddings, and about the simple but harsh life in Mexico. *Dichos* were passed down from generation to generation and my abuelita, Maria Luna, absorbed them, made them her own, and passed them on to my father.

Doña Tánis was a great parent according to my grandmother. She was also a bit timid around my great-grandfather Cesario. He was a *gritón* (yelled loudly when upset) like my grandfather Pedro. Tánislada died on April 1, 1927 at about the age of 80.

Great-grandfather Cesario collapsed at the dinner table from a heart attack in 1917 at age 72, when Tío Julio was 25 years old.

Family Roots in Solomonville, Arizona

The Escobedo's settled in Solomonville (now known as Solomon), Arizona. Many of my relatives still live there. Solomonville is a small rural, unincorporated community east of Safford in Graham County, Arizona. The residents are predominantly Mexican-American.

Solomon's history can be described as follows:

"The community's origins go back to the indigenous peoples of the region. Little is known of its history prior to the coming of the Europeans. In the Early 19th century, settlers who fit the modern term Hispanic came to the region. They named the town they founded "Pueblo Viejo" (Old Pueblo) because of the previous Native American settlement, the ruins of which are still visible.

In the 1870's Mormons moved to the region. The town is named after Isadore Elkan Solomon, a Jewish, German immigrant who came to the town in the 1870's. Mr. Solomon was searching for a place to start up a business and when he arrived, there were only five residences in the town." [1]

According to an article in The New Vision, Our Lady of Guadalupe Church was built in 1884 in Solomonville, 28 years before Arizona became a state. Our Lady of Guadalupe Parish was formally dedicated in 1891. My parents were married there and I was baptized there. I also went to Sunday mass with my Grandma Maria and my Godmother and Aunt, Isabel Escobedo Ornelas. I have very special memories of this church as it was the place where my spiritual roots began.

I lived in Solomonville as a toddler and attended the first grade at the small elementary school. We lived near my grandparents and I was fortunate to visit them often. My cousin Jessie Escobedo Formica also lived there, and raised her children at Tía Maria and Tío Tomas' home. Jessie shared the following memories of Solomonville:

---

1 http://en.wikipedia.org/wiki/Solomon,_Arizona. Retrieved April 4, 2017.

"The small town of Solomonville had a large store owned by Mr. I.E. Solomon and Mr. Wickersham, called the Wickersham Commercial Store. There was a hotel, and the first bank built was the Gila Bank, which later became the first Valley National Bank in Arizona. It is currently Chase Bank. The drug store was owned by Hal Empie, who later became a great Arizona artist. He died in the late 1990's in Tubac, Arizona. His daughter still has an art gallery in Tubac, which sells Mr. Empie's art. Solomonville was the Graham County and Greenlee County seat for many years and after the railroad by-passed the town, the Graham County seat was moved to Safford, Arizona and the Greenlee County seat was moved to Clifton, Arizona.

Life in Solomonville was peaceful. It was comprised of mostly Mexican-American families who spoke Spanish, and it was the children's first language. They learned English from the older siblings and at school.

The homes were all constructed in adobe brick and most had patios of hard watered down dirt, swept and cleaned daily. Each home had flowers, vines, mulberry trees and vegetable gardens. Neighbors shared their food, their joys, their woes and everyone knew each other."

Virgen de Guadalupe Church, founded in 1884.

Pedro Chavez Escobedo and Maria Luna

Grandma Maria married Pedro Chavez Escobedo in the Virgen de Guadalupe Catholic Church in Solomonville, Arizona on April 23, 1916. She was 17 and grandpa was 20. They had seven children—Juanita, Cesario, Carmen, Isabel, Beatrice, Pedro, Jr., and Raymundo. My Tío Ray is the only sibling still living.

Grandma Maria was a devoted wife and mother. She was just under five-feet tall, slender, had dark skin and wore gray rimmed glasses. She used to call me her *"negrita del jabón,"* because I have dark skin like hers. She derived this name from the cover of a bar of soap that had a picture of a little black girl. I took it as a term of endearment.

I loved to watch her comb her long gray hair, braid it, wrap it up in a small bun at the nape of her neck, and anchor it with brown tortoise shell combs. When I visited her, I enjoyed watching her make flour tortillas on her wood-burning stove. I still remember that rich smell. And no one could make refried pinto beans like Grandma Maria.

When my brothers and I were toddlers, mom and dad would visit our grandparents often. My mom told me that during one of our visits, my grandfather ran to his garden, picked a big watermelon and proceeded to crack it open for us. My grandmother got upset and yelled, *"¿Viejo indecente, qué no ves que la Bri tiene los niños limpios? Se van a ensuciar."* (You crazy man, can't you see that Bri has the children dressed up and clean? They are going to get dirty.) Grandpa just smirked and gave us a red, juicy piece of watermelon anyway.

My grandparent's eldest daughter, Juanita, died quite young at childbirth. Juanita had four girls—Nora, Amelia, Mary Lou and little Juanita (also known as "Baby"). Juanita died when her youngest ("Baby") was born. Baby Juanita arrived two months early and weighed a mere two and a half pounds. Occasionally she was placed in a small shoe box to sleep. I learned that Uncle Ray (then ten years old) awoke from his sleep when he heard a cry. He thought it was his cat meowing and placed the shoe box outdoors! Once grandma found out, he was in big trouble. My abuelitos raised "Baby" until she married in 1956.

My grandparent's marriage was challenging. Grandma Maria endured my grandfather's drinking and womanizing. Divorce was unheard of back then. She was determined to keep the family intact. Due to her emotional suffering, she instilled in my father the importance of respecting his wife and honoring his marriage.

Abuelita died of ruptured ulcers when I was in the eighth grade. While on her sick bed, she told my grandfather that she would give him five years of fun, and then he would join her. My grandmother died on September 22, 1961 and grandfather died exactly five years later, on September 22, 1966.

Top: Phelps Dodge copper miners. Pedro Escobedo, Jr. seated third on the right.

Right: Pedro Escobedo, Jr. U.S. Army, 1946.

Pedro Escobedo, Jr. Family History

My "*padrecito*," Pedro Luna Escobedo, Jr., was born on April 4, 1924. He only completed an eighth-grade education, and enlisted in the U.S. Army at age 18. He served in World War II and was assigned as a Military Police at a Japanese internment camp in the state of Washington. He was also assigned to a team of engineers to clean up the surrounding cities in Japan followed by the devastation caused by the atomic bomb on Hiroshima.

While in the Army, he studied agriculture. He came from a family of farmers and had a passion for cultivating the land and growing cotton, chili, melons, corn and vegetables. After his honorable discharge, he married Brijida Barela on April 2, 1948, and worked in the cotton farms in Solomonville and Safford, Arizona. As our family grew, he realized he needed to earn more so he applied to work in the copper mines in nearby Morenci.

In 1953, when I turned four years old, he got a job as a track laborer at the Phelps Dodge copper mine in Morenci, Arizona. Later, he became the first supervisor to have a woman employee in his work group. This created a great challenge as he had to contend with a motley, foul-mouthed crew. He demanded respect from the men and modeled that behavior. He was a brilliant, hard-working man who supported and loved his family in countless ways. His sense of humor and talent for storytelling attracted friends from throughout southern Arizona. His ethical way of living brought him respect from co-workers, relatives and acquaintances. He retired from Phelps Dodge after 33 years of service.

My four brothers, Anthony, Edward, Benjamin, Pedro Escobedo III, and I are the recipients of the lessons we learned from our parents, and we carry them on as best we can.

Cesario Escobedo Family

Cesario Escobedo (1845-1917)

Romana Chavez Escobedo

Carmen Escobedo

Tánislada Luna (1845-1927)
(Common law wife)

Pedro Escobedo

Rosalia Luna

Tomás Escobedo

Maria Luna (1889-1961)

José Escobedo

Julio Escobedo

Pedro Chavez Escobedo Family

Pedro Chavez Escobedo (1886-1966)   Maria Luna Escobedo (1889-1961)

Cesario Escobedo
Nicolasa Lopez

Juanita Escobedo
Procopio Montoya

Carmen Escobedo
Fred Montez/Ben Salas

Isabel Escobedo
Gregorio Ornelas

Beatrice Escobedo
Salvador Ruiz

Pedro Escobedo, Jr.
Brijida Barela

Raymundo Escobedo
Ophelia Ruiz/Mary Sanchez

Pedro Escobedo, Jr. Family

Pedro Escobedo, Jr. (1924-2001)

Brijida Barela (1929)

Anthony Escobedo (1950-2007)
Kerry Peggy (divorced)
Shawnda
Kay Razo (divorced)
Lisa, Jacob and Justin

Geneva Escobedo (1949)
Joseph Duarte (divorced)
Rome, Yvette and Candice
(step- daughters)

Benjamin Escobedo (1953)
Natalie Tally (not wed)
Benjamin Escobedo, Jr.

Edward Escobedo (1952)
Josephine Benavidez
Michael, Eric, and April

Pedro Escobedo III (1956)
JoAnn Guerra (divorced)
Rhianna

Julio Escobedo Family

Julio Escobedo (1892-1976)

Petra Hernandez (1901-1996)

Julio Escobedo, Jr.
Mary Jo Garcia
Jon Julio, Carla, Dee, and Julie

Herlinda Escobedo
Edmundo Limón
Alma

Romana Escobedo
Roger Lee/Ernest Forsythe
Yolanda

Manuela "Nellie" Escobedo
Mike Plasencio
Joseph, Lucy Michele,
Felisa, and Peter James

Gloria Escobedo
Louis Campos
Deborah, Louis Keith, Glenn
Michael, Lee Christopher,
Carol, and Carla

Margarita Escobedo
Frank Wulftange
Frank Gregory, Margarita
and Romanita

Pedro Escobedo, Jr. U.S. Army Photo 1946.

Pedro, My Little Father

In honor of my father, I share this poem I wrote and read at his eulogy on June 19, 2001:

I dedicate these words to my
beloved father.
A worker of strength and dedication.
He taught me the most important
things in life—
To love family and to express love.

Pedro, my little father...
With your wonderful personality,
your talent to make us all laugh.
Your stories and your *dichos*
will always be remembered.

Pedro, my little father
with that short little body
with a round belly
and that little bald head
will never be forgotten.

Pedro, my little father
That brilliant smile that
shines like the stars, and
at times I feel him by my side.

Pedro, my little father
I remember the moment of
your golden wedding anniversary
when you danced with mom,
how handsome you looked.

Pedro, my little father
I miss your advice and
your love songs.
Pedro, my little father
Tell us a joke.

Pedrito Padrecito

Estas palabras se las dedico
a mi querido Padrecito.
Un trabajador de fuerza y dedicación.
Él me enseño lo más importante
de la vida—
Querer a la familia y expresar cariño.

Pedrito, Padrecito…
Con su genio fabuloso,
su talento para hacernos reír.
Sus cuentos y sus dichos
se recordarán.

Pedrito, Padrecito
con su cuerpecito chapito
con panzita,
y su cabezita peloncita
nunca se olvidarán.

Pedrito, Padrecito
Su sonrisa brillosa como
las estrellas, y
a veces lo siento a mi lado.

Pedrito, Padrecito
Recuerdo el momento de tu
boda de oro.
cuando bailaste con Mamá,
qué guapo te veías.

Pedrito, Padrecito
extraño tus consejos y
tus canciones de amor.
Pedrito, Padrecito
cuéntanos un chiste.

Epilogue

This book has been a labor of love to write. I hope that it will be shared with the younger generation of Escobedos, so that they become familiar with our Mexican heritage and our family history. It is important to pass on family values to each generation. I am so proud to have been born an Escobedo and to stand on the shoulders of my great-grandparents, grandparents and parents.

As a tribute to my father, the inspiration for this book, I asked my baby brother, Pedro Escobedo III, to share a poem he wrote for Dad on one of his birthdays. The title "Doc" was selected because my Dad used to engage in self-diagnosis and consult medical encyclopedias to determine what he thought ailed him. "Doc" was the nickname my brother Pete gave him. Every time he visited dad he greeted him with, "What's up Doc?"

Doc

The thin haired man with so much knowledge
would have sent us to the finest college.

He always taught us right from wrong and to this day, we get along.
To be close and never lie, be yourself, and always try.

The thin haired man, his name was Dad, the finest father
a child could have.

We love this guy with Clark Gable ears, the thin haired man,
throughout the years.

www.ingramcontent.com/pod-product-compliance
Lightning Source LLC
Chambersburg PA
CBHW060811090426
42737CB00002B/35

9 781936 885237